Miracle
Signs and Wonders from God

Miraculous Bodily Phenomena!

By

Michael Freze, S.F.O.

Copyright © 2016 by Michael Freze, S,F.O.
All Rights Reserved

Any Scripture quotations referenced are from the New Revised Standard Version Bible: Catholic Edition (Copyright © 1993) by the Division of Christian Education of the National Council of the Churches of Christ in the U.S.A. Used by permission. All rights reserved.

Permission to publish originally granted at Helena, Montana, by Most Reverend Elden F. Curtiss, now former Bishop of Helena, Montana (since appointed Archbishop of Omaha, Nebraska). **Permission to publish is a statement that the book is free from doctrinal and moral error.** No implication is contained therein that the one granting the permission agrees with the contents, opinions, or statements expressed.

"Blessed are those who have not seen and yet believe" (Jn 20:29).

"To all Christian believers for whom no explanation is necessary because of their great faith; and to all those who do not believe, where no explanation will suffice…" (Michael Freze, S.F.O.)

Table of Contents

Acknowledgments	5
Foreword	7
Bodily Phenomena	14
General Overview	14
Types of Bodily Phenomena	18
Liquefaction	18
Levitation	21
Bilocation	23
Transverberation	26
Sacred Stigmata	32
Incorruptibility	41
Additional Information	43
Luminous Effluvia	48
Heavenly Aromas	51
Mysterious Oils	53
Resurrections	54
About the Author	62
My Religious eBooks In Print	64

Educational Background	67
Television Appearances	68
Links To My National TV Appearances	68
Links To My Writing Sites	69

Acknowledgments

I would like to thank Father Patrick Patton, formerly of the Diocese of Helena, Montana, for his long-time support of my writing apostolate. Father Patton has been a good friend and director of my spiritual development for many years in the past. He was always there to offer his theological advice on various issues related to my earlier works. Father Patton is fluent in several languages and has been an immense help in translating many of my sources for a number of my earlier works with Our Sunday Visitor: *They Bore the Wounds of Christ: The Mystery of the Sacred Stigmata* (1989), *The Making of Saints* (1991), and *Patron Saints* (1992). Father Patton is very knowledgeable in issues related to Church history, spirituality, and dogmatic theology. He had been an Army chaplain for many years and has served as a parish priest in the Diocese of Helena.

I thank the Most Reverend Elden F. Curtiss (who was the Bishop of Helena until he was named Archbishop of Omaha on June 25, 1993) for his past support of my writing career. Bishop Curtiss is a respected theologian and has been active and influential in various bishops' conferences around the United States. He has reviewed a number of writings over the course of the years.

Once again, I must thank two priests who became dear friends of mine years ago: Fathers Joseph Pius Martin, O.F.M. Cap., and Alessio Parente, O.F.M. Cap., of San Giovanni Rotondo, near Foggia, Italy. These two friars were close friends of Padre Pio for years and were very involved with his earlier cause of canonization. Father Joseph and Father Alessio helped me enormously with my first two books published by Our Sunday

Visitor. I had the privilege of visiting both priests in the summers of 1988 and 1990, where I received hours of taped interviews and written materials related to the topics of those two works. I have indirectly relied on those earlier insights for my recent books as well.

To all the staff at Our Sunday Visitor, I extend my deepest appreciation for their support of my work during their initial publications. I am particularly indebted to then president and publisher, Robert P. Lockwood. Our Sunday Visitor is one of the finest Catholic publishing houses in the world, and one of the largest as well. I am proud to have contributed to this great organization.

Foreword

When writing a book that deals with extraordinary supernatural phenomena, one must take particular care in describing events and experiences in such a way that does not run contrary to the official teachings of the Church. This is especially true with the Roman Catholic faith, which exercises prudence and caution concerning all aspects related to supernatural and/or extraordinary matters.

However, prudence and caution does not exempt one from writing or talking about unusual experiences that affect millions of Christians throughout the world. Indeed, to deliberately remain ignorant or to purposely deny God's extraordinary works in our world today is a sign of irresponsibility toward one's faith life, spiritual journey, and knowledge about the Christian faith.

In 1966, former Pope Paul VI abolished two former canons of the 1917 Code of Canon Law (revised in 1983) that dealt with such matters. These were Canons 1399 and 2318, respectively. Pope Paul, recognizing the importance of not despising prophecy but testing everything and holding fast to what is good (1 Thes 5:19-21), followed the wisdom of Pope Urban VIII (1623-1644), who once declared this about supernatural experiences: "In cases which concern private revelations, it is better to believe than not to believe, for, if you believe, and it is proven true, you will be happy that you have believed, because our Holy Mother asked it. If you believe, and it should be proven false, you will receive all blessings as if had been true, because you believed it to be true."

Although we are now free to study, write, or speak about supernatural experiences in the lives of the faithful, nevertheless Pope Urban VIII made it clear that all beliefs in such experiences are based upon mere human credibility-not divine faith. With this is mind, I offer you, the faithful, this work on supernatural experiences in the life of the Church.

In conformity with Pope Urban VIII (and every Holy Father since), I resign final judgment related to all mystical or supernatural experiences to the ultimate judgment and supreme wisdom of the official teachings and/or recommendations of the Roman Catholic Church. Until that time, we are free to believe or not believe according to the dictates of our will and informed conscience any particular phenomenon that has yet to be officially confirmed.

(Incidentally, the reader may notice what might seem to be misspellings of or inconsistencies in the names of saints, places, etc.-hey are simply variants of the same names. Moreover, dates and details of events appearing in this work may not coincide with those found in other works. The reason for this is be cause in many cases historians do not agree with one another on such things, thus the seeming discrepancies. It should also be mentioned that, depending on the source used some individuals cited will have only their last names or their first names used in this book).

The Roman Catholic Church is blessed to have such a rich tradition that spans nearly two thousand years. During the course of this time, a vast array of topics has been written on all aspects of the Christian faith, among them Church history; biblical archaeology; papal history; patristic studies concerning the early Church Fathers; hagiology; moral, dogmatic, historical, philosophical, spiritual, and biblical theology; biblical criticism; and Church law.

Perhaps one of the more fascinating and mysterious areas of Catholic theology is that which deals with mysticism and mystical phenomena: miracles, healings, signs, wonders, prophecy, voices, visions, apparitions, locutions, and extraordinary charisms.

There are few (if any) other religions that have so many writings, teachings, and personal anecdotes based upon the supernatural life and the extraordinary experiences associated with it. Indeed, that is one of the things that makes the Catholic faith so rich: the belief that we as Church are not separated or isolated from the divine; that our God includes us in His master plan and intervenes in our lives on a personal and intimate basis. Without this concept of the human-divine relationship, much would be lost in the Catholic faith, which perceives itself to be a body of Christ, a family of God.

We are a people of faith who believe in Jesus Christ as the God-man, fully human and fully divine. The God of our fathers has preordained that He would intervene in human history by relating to the human person in the most significant and meaningful way known: to take upon Himself the flesh of humanity while maintaining His divinity throughout: Christ Jesus, who, though he was in the form of God, ... emptied himself, being born in the likeness of men" (Phil 2:5-7).

If God really decided that we should be made in His image (Gn 1:26), then it stands to reason that we are to share most intimately in that supernatural life through the gift of His most perfect grace that moves and sustains us through His Spirit: "By this we know that we abide in him and he in us, because he has given us his own Spirit" (1 Jn 4:13).

It is the life in the Spirit, then, that compels the Catholic to seek the Lord beginning with this earthly life; it is the eternal presence of the Spirit that allows us to enjoy the beatific vision in the eternal life hereafter.

Because the Catholic understands this deep and intimate relationship with God and His Spirit, he or she also knows or at least senses that there is more to this life than what readily meets the eye. We know that, at certain times with different people, God chooses to reveal Himself: he who loves me will be loved by my Father, and I will love him and manifest myself to him" (Jn 14:21). How does this manifestation take place? According to St. Paul, it can occur through "signs and wonders and various miracles and by gifts of the Holy Spirit" (Heb 2:4).

In the Book of Revelation, we know from John's writing that the supernatural manifests through voices and visions: "I was in the Spirit on the Lord's day, and I heard behind me a loud voice like a trumpet saying, 'Write what you see in a book and send it to the seven churches" (Rv 1:10-11); "Then I turned to see the voice that was speaking to me" (Rv 1:12).

We also know from this same book that even angels appear to man from time to time: "I John am he who heard and saw these things. And when I heard and saw them, I fell down to worship at the feet of the angel who showed them to me" (Rv 22:8). Or again, in the Gospel of Luke, we are told that "the angel Gabriel was sent from God to a city of Galilee named Nazareth, to a virgin betrothed to a man whose name was Joseph" (Lk 1:26-27). In Matthew, we see the same experience, in which "an angel of the Lord appeared to Joseph in a dream" (Mt 2:13).

These are but many of the many Scripture passages-both Old and New-that refer explicitly to God's direct intervention in human affairs through voices, visions, and apparitions. It occurs so often, in fact, that one must be doubtful of the very credibility of the critics and skeptics who continue to write off these passages (and the hundreds of documented cases in the post-Apostolic era) as something symbolic, spiritual, or mythical in nature. These same critics-the so-called "new," or liberal, theologians-also have a habit of writing off many other things pertaining to the supernatural order: angels, demons, heaven, hell, purgatory, etc. Perhaps they are afraid of taking anything literally or at face value; after all, that seems too simple or naive.

Let us remember, however, that it is much more difficult to be simple than to be complicated. As any professional writer or public speaker if this is true! True genius, talent, and great intellect are often disguised in very deceptively simple terms that provide a profound depth of wisdom, truth, and understanding. Take Jesus Christ and His teachings as an example. Whoever claims that those simple parables are childish or shallow is kidding himself! Simple? Yes. Simplistic? Let's put it this way: Only a fool would measure Christ's words in terms of their obvious simplicity. Each of His teachings contains a mine full of wisdom . Perhaps that is why little children understand so well: They have not forgotten to be open to the spirit of truth. It is only the intellectuals of the world who lose that sense of dimension and wonder because they are too conditioned by their own thoughts.

This is a work that focuses on the supernatural phenomena experienced throughout the life of the Catholic Church.

Obviously, the topic of the supernatural is too large to include everything in a single volume such as this. Indeed, it would take dozens of volumes to cover all aspects and phases of these manifestations associated with the mystical life or supernatural states.

Therefore, this work should be considered as an overview designed to give the reader a general background on the treatment of the supernatural experience. Presenting the material in this fashion requires careful selection from the thousands of written sources and documents the Church has gathered over the past two millennia. Clearly, only key examples may be included in a work of this nature.

I have tried to limit my sources to those that can be verified through Sacred Scripture, eyewitnesses, lengthy documentation, or through the teachings of the magisterium. In addition, I rely upon such sources as the wisdom of the saints and the great mystics of the Church. Although not doctrinal in nature, these teachings or examples serve to help us better understand the personal nature of these experiences from those highly esteemed in the Church.

On occasion, I have used non-Catholic sources in parts of this work but only from reliable, well-known experts in their respected fields. Even then, the non-Catholic sources are kept to a minimum in order to remain true to a Catholic approach to this topic.

The nature of this topic demands a prudent and cautious approach. The words "supernatural" and "miracle" have been over-worked and abused by many throughout history, so a serious attempt has been made to give as balanced a view as possible.

It is difficult (if not impossible) to present the "perfect work" on mystical phenomena or the supernatural life, mainly because the realm of the supernatural is oftentimes unexplainable using mere human words. Furthermore, not everyone who is a true Christian can claim direct experience in these areas. Finally, even those who are extraordinarily blessed by God with the supernatural life fall far short in understanding all of the mysteries of faith, as great saints and mystics themselves have admitted.

Nevertheless, we must continue to try to understand the divine mysteries in order to grow in our faith and draw closer to God. For it is only through seeking the Lord that we might find Him; we must "call upon him while he is near" (Is 55:6). And never is God more intimately present to us than through His intervention in our personal lives. That is the meaning and purpose of supernatural manifestations-voices, visions, apparitions, signs, and wonders which occur to the faithful from time to time. God still moves among us, and by doing so shows us that we are never completely alone in this earthly pilgrimage, which we must patiently endure.

Bodily Phenomena
General Overview

Many unusual physical phenomena occur in the lives of the saints, as if these were marks or signs of God's special grace-the "visible credentials" of predilection. In these holy victims, the laws of nature appear to be suspended; the scientific and medical worlds have been unable to explain the operations that lay behind these mysterious occurrences. Yet they have been authenticated through intensive observations under close scrutiny, whether it be in their home or in the hospital.

One of the bodily phenomena that has occurred in these saintly souls is that which is called the **gift of perfume**, also known as the **odor of sanctity**. It involves the heavenly scent that issues forth from the body, a sweet and desirable scent often compared to the smell of fresh roses. Listen to the words of St. John of the Cross:

"He (Jesus) makes her so beautiful and rich and so imbues her with delights that it seems to her she rests upon a bed, made of a variety of sweet divine flowers, that. delights with its touch and refreshes with its fragrance" (*The Spiritual Canticle*, Stanza 24.)

Or again we hear him say:

"Sometimes the fragrance is so abundant that it seems to the soul she is clothed with delight and bathed in inestimable glory, to such an extent that the experience is not only within her but overflows and becomes manifest outside of her, and those capable of recognizing it are aware of her experience. It seems to them that he is in a pleasant garden filled with the delights and riches of God..." (*The Spiritual Canticle*, Stanza 17.)

Of course, these descriptions by the mystical Doctor are taken from the mystical Song of Songs: "Awake, O north wind, and come, O south wind! Blow upon my garden, let its fragrance be wafted abroad. Let my beloved come to his garden, and eat its choicest fruits" (Sg 4:16); "the scent of your garments is the scent of Lebanon" (Sg 4: 11); "I will lie me to the mountains of myrrh and the hills of frankincense. You are all-fair, my love; there is no flaw in you" (Sg 4.6-7), etc.

This is aroma has been observed in some of the stigmatists while they were living (especially noticeable from the wounds themselves), and in others it is emitted after death directly from the body or from the site of the grave. In some cases (such as with Padre Pio and Therese Neumann), the scent is smelled as a sign of their presence, usually from bilocation, but sometimes after death when they come to the aid of a soul in need. At other times, the aroma stays for a length of time in a particular place that the stigmatist has visited or lived-a corridor, a room or even a church. Some who have touched the perfumed stigmatist have been known to carry the same scent on them, as if the stigmatist's "traces" were momentarily left in their midst.

Some of these victims were known for the sweet scented wounds which they possessed: St. Humiliane, St. Ida of Louvain, Dominic dei Paradise, Jeannie Marie de la Croix, as well as Padre Pio of Pietrelcina. Others emitted the powerful but pleasant aroma after their deaths: St. Teresa of Avila, St. Rose of Lima, and Blessed Catherine dei Racconigi, to name a few. These scents are reaffirmations that the wounds are of a supernatural origin, for normal wounds tend to fester and leave foul odors.

St. Teresa of Avila (1515-82) carried a sweet fragrance throughout her life and even after her death. Teresa's cell room was saturated with this heavenly aroma, and reports of her grave giving off the same scent are well known. In fact, when this stigmatist's body was exhumed on July 4, 1583, Father Jerome Gracian, provincial of her Carmelite Order, noticed a strong but beautiful fragrance which lasted several days. As late as 1914, when Teresa's heart wound was examined by the sisters at Alba de Tormes, they noticed the same delicate scent coming from Teresa's incorruptible body.

St. Catherine dei Ricci (1522-90), the holy stigmatized Dominican, was reported to have given off a flowery scent at the time of her death.

Many other saintly persons-stigmatist and non-stigmatist-have been known for their sweet bodily aroma: Pope Marcel, St. Aldegonde, St Menard, St. Dominic. St. Catherine of Bologna, Blessed Lucy of Narni, Blessed Catherine dei Racconigi, St. Claire dei Rimini, St. Fine of Tuscany, St. Elizabeth of Portugal, St. Rose of Lima, St. Louis Bertrand, St. Joseph dei Copertino, St. Thomas of Villanova, St. Raymond dei Pennafort, St. Willibrod, St. Agnes of Montepulciano, and St. Mary Magdalen dei Pazzi are among the many of such privileged souls.

The **gift of perfume** is not the only bodily phenomena known in the lives of the stigmatists. Another mysterious one is the **lack of sleep** that some of these souls have experienced. Padre Pio was reported to have slept only a few hours each night. He would often study and pray until one o'clock in the morning, then arise at three o'clock to prepare for his 5:00 a.m. Mass! St. Catherine dei Ricci slept for one one hour every week. Others, such as St. Catherine of Siena and Therese Neumann, required little sleep as well.

Many of thes victims' bodies were re-established in youth and beauty after their death, such as St. Francis of Assisi, St. Catherine of Siena, St. Catherine dei Ricci, St. Mary Magdalen dei Pazzi, and St. Rose of Lin remarkable when one considers how much abuse and torment their bodies and souls went through as expiatory victims!

Another unusual phenomenon of the body was seen in Padre of Pietrelcina. The stigmatized friar had often been sick with extremely high fevers. When others tried to take his body temperature, the thermometer would break on occasion because of the unusually high readings: a temperature of 120-125 degrees was often reported through reliable sources! Of course, this cannot be explained by any natural means. The temptation would be to discredit such stories because we often tend to think in terms of human reason or the natural order. But these mystical charisms are above the natural order, given by the hand of God to His chosen instruments. Again, we must conclude that the extraordinary gifts that each stigmatist seems to possess in abundance are signs of God's special privileges in His favored souls, especially those who follow the Cross of His Son in order to co-operate in the redemptive plan of the world.

Types of Bodily Phenomena

Liquefaction

Many unusual bodily phenomena have occurred to various privileged soul throughout the history of the Church. One of the most unusual phenomena is known as liquefaction: the experience whereby a preserved deceased person's blood loses its hard, crumb like characteristics and miraculously changes back into liquid as fresh as it was when that person was alive.

Our first example of this type of phenomenon revolves around a St. Nazarius of m (d. c. [died circa] 68), who was beheaded in Milan for preaching the faith during the persecutions of Emperor Nero. A legend says that Nazarius was taught by St. Peter during his time in the City of Seven Hills. Tradition claims that St. Ambrose found Nazarius' remains in Milan in A.D. 395 and had them preserved there in a shrine. Witnesses reported that his blood was still liquid with a fresh, red color several hundred years after his death. The feast day of St. Nazarius is July 28.

Perhaps the best-known case of liquefaction is found in the tradition of St. Januarius (d. c. 305) of Naples, Italy. This martyr was imprisoned with Festus and Desiderius by the governor of Campania for witnessing to the faith. Eventually, Januarius was beheaded near Pozzouli. Devotees of Januarius preserved some of his blood in a vial. It is claimed that during the past four centuries, the remains of his hardened blood has bubbled and boiled when the vial is exposed in the cathedral at Naples. Although extensively investigated by scientists and Church authorities, no rational explanation has ever come forth for this extraordinary phenomenon. To this day, St. Januarius is considered the patron of blood banks. His feast is celebrated on September 19.

St. Pantaleon (d. c. 305) of Nicomedia was eventually martyred for his faith. It is reported that ever since he was beheaded under the orders of Emperor Diocletian, his blood has liquefied on his annual feast day of July 27. Pantaleon is called the Wonder Worker in the East and the Great Martyr. He is one of the Fourteen Holy Helpers.

The saintly soul Patricia of Constantinople (d. c. 665) moved to Italy to avoid marriage and to preserve her virginity. In Rome, she consecrated herself to God. After her death in Naples, it is claimed that her blood, which is preserved in a vial there, still liquefies some thirteen hundred years after her death. St. Patricia's feast day is celebrated on August 25.

Another example of the phenomenon of liquefaction occurred in the preserved blood of St. Andrew Avellino (1521-1608) from Castronuovo, Italy. Andrew was a great missionary to the people of Naples, Italy, where he eventually served as a superior of the Theatines. After his death, his blood, according to many witnesses, was said to liquefy and bubble. However, the local Monsignor Giovanni Pamfili (who later became Pope Innocent X) refused to believe the claims.

Bernardino Realino (1530-1616) from Capri, Italy, became a Jesuit and later worked in Naples. His reputation for sanctity soon spread throughout the region. Six years before he died, the blood from an unhealed leg wound was collected by the local people in memory of their saint. Witnesses over the next two hundred fifty years claimed that Bernardino's preserved blood remained liquefied and was seen to bubble and boil. Pope Pius XII canonized Bernardino in 1947. His feast day is July 3.

Levitation

Levitation-the mystical bodily phenomenon whereby a person is literally and physically lifted off the ground in a type of ecstatic trance-has fascinated the faithful for centuries. Thi is partly due to the fact that there are so many authentic levitations that have been documented in the lives of the saints. When a soul is enraptured in the presence of God, he or she sometimes experiences what is known as the **mystical flight** (also known as **transportation**, **teletransportation**, or **aerial flights**). When this occurs, the privileged soul is lifted up from one location and moved to another. This mystical swoon is similar to the gift of **bilocation**, whereby a person appears in more than one place at the same time. The difference with the latter is that the person is still physically present in the original location; with the former, that person is moved to another place ,even if momentarily.

St. Milburga (d. c. 722) was known for her holiness. Many witnesses claimed to have seen her levitate on frequent occasions. Her feast is celebrated on February 23.

One of the most famous examples of this gift of levitation is found in the life of St. Christina the Astonishing (1150-1224) from Brusthem, Belgium. When she was about twenty-one, Christina was seen by her entire congregation levitating to the ceiling of her church during the Sacrifice of the Mass. This occurred during a Mass being offered for her, since it was presumed that she was very ill and approaching death. Her pastor ordered her to come down, and she did so at once under holy obedience. Later, Christina claimed that she was given a vision of heaven, hell, and purgatory during this momentary flight. It is reported many other times that Christina was seen levitating to the church rafters in an experience similar to this one. Her feast day is July 24.

Blessed Lodovica Albertoni (1473-1533) of Rome, Italy, was seen to levitate frequently during the last years of her life while immersed in the state of prayer. This Third Order Franciscan was beatified by Pope Clement X in 1671.

It is believed that St. Martin de Porres (1579-1639) of Lima, Peru, was endowed with many supernatural gifts, such as bilocation and transportation. He was canonized by Pope John XXIII in 1962. He is the patron of interracial justice.

St. Joseph of Cupertino, Italy (1603-1663), is another example of a well-documented case. It is said that there were witnesses to over seventy levitations of this beloved saint. Pope Urban VIII reported to have favored the extraordinary experiences of this man from Cupertino. He was canonized in 1767 and is known as the patron saint of air travelers and pilots.

St. Benedict Joseph Labre (1748-1783) of Amettes, France, "the beggar of Rome," was privileged to receive many supernatural gifts. It is reported he frequently levitated and was known to have bilocated on numerous occasions as well. He was canonized in 1883 by Pope Leo XIII.

Bilocation

Another extraordinary supernatural experience is that of **bilocation**, whereby a person is physically seen in two different places at one time. Although incredible as this may seem, it is a common gift of the mystics in the Church.

It is claimed that Venerable Anne Catherine Emmerich (1774-1824), famed visionary and stigmatic of the Church, bilocated frequently. Anne claimed that her guardian angel led her to the places where she was transported. Many of these mystical journeys led to places in the Holy Land during the life and times of Jesus and the Apostles. These visions are described in the two volume work *The Life of Anne Catherine Emmerich* by Father Carl E. Schmoger.

Lucia dos Santos was one of the three young visionaries who claimed to have seen the Blessed Virgin Mary at Fatima, Portugal, in 1917. It is reported that her cousin once was lost for week until Jacinta Marto (1910-1920), another of the seers, prayed for his soul. Within a few days, the cousin was home. The story related by Lucia claims that the young boy had stolen money from his parents, went on a spending spree, then ran away from home. Soon, he became lost and prayed for guidance. Jacinta appeared to him and led him on the road to his home.

In a diary kept by Father Joseph Naber, the parish priest of Konnersreuth, Bavaria, Germany, and director of Therese

Neumann (1898-1962) for many years, it was written on May 8, 1931, that a complete stranger had contemplated suicide because of an economic crisis. Suddenly, Therese Neumann appeared to him and warned him not to take his own life. The man converted and changed his mind about committing suicide. Therese later said that her guardian angel assumed Therese's form to save the suicidal man.

Adrienne von Speyr (1902-1967), lay stigmatist and spiritual child of renowned Swiss theologian Hans Urs von Balthasar (who died in 1988), was blessed with the gift of bilocation. Adrienne claimed to bilocate to the Nazi concentration camps during World War II in order to comfort the suffering there. She was also transported to seminaries, abandoned churches, and various convents throughout the world. Adrienne claimed that she was guided by her guardian angel through many of these visitations. Although some discard the authenticity of bilocation altogether, it is difficult to ignore the testimony of many serious and brilliant scholars who believe in such a phenomenon. One of the most respected, of course is Hans von Balthasar, a world-renowned theologian and a favorite of former Pope John Paul II. Shortly before his death, he was made a cardinal by Pope John Paul but died before he could assume his office. Hans once wrote the life story of this remarkable woman, and had published a number of the many books she had written.

Although Padre Pio of Pietrelcina (1887-1968) never left Our Lady of Grace Friary in San Giovanni Rotondo, Italy, between 1918 and 1968 (except for going to the polls to vote), he was seen in numerous places throughout all those years by people far from the friary.

Marthe Robin (1902-1981), lay mystic and stigmatic from France, reportedly bilocated. A story is told about how Marthe, though bedridden at her home in Chateauneuf de Galure, knew about every detail of her mother's operation in the hospital at Lyons. Her mother needed surgery for an intestinal disorder. When speaking to her later, Marthe astonished the doctors, who were amazed to find that every detail Marthe reported was accurate.

Transverberation

The mystical wounds of love (of the soul or heart) are wounds that transform the victim soul into a receptacle of divine love. With these living flames of love, the soul is transported to an intensely intimate relationship with God. Normally, these wounds precede the impression of the stigmata upon the body or soul; they are a kind of preparation for the eventual and complete transformation of the victim into another Christ crucified ... a living crucifix of redemptive love.

Technically, this phenomenom has been called **transverberation** of the heart. Some mystics have even experienced what is known as the **exchange of hearts**, whereby the Lord consumes the heart of the victim with the fire of His Sacred Heart, and the Lord likewise makes the heart of the victim His own.

Because the wound of love is a forerunner to the impression of the Five Wounds of the Sacred Stigmata, we need to take a closer look at what this wound does to the soul, and how it is initially received.

Before the wound appears, the victim has normally achieved a high degree of perfection, including advanced states of mystical experience. Indeed, few are the number who have reached this level and have been found worthy to receive such extraordinary graces.

Normally, the wound is given during the state of ecstasy, where the mystic is completely absorbed in the divine love, oblivious to all surroundings. He or she appears to be caught up in a different dimension of time and space, a state that betrays all normal human experience.

Blessed Angela of Foligno (1248-1309), holy victim of our Lord's love expressed this state in the following manner:

When the soul is elevated above itself, and, illuminated by the presence of God, enters into intimate communication with Him, it knows, enjoys and rests in a divine happiness which it cannot express, for it surpasses every word and every concept. Each ecstasy is a new ecstasy and all the ecstasies together are one inex pressible thing ....

After the victim experiences this level of mystical ecstasy, a heavenly being sent by God, or even the Lord himself, may pay a visit to this victim and impart a permanent wound in the heart or the soul by means of a spear, dart or arrow. St. Teresa of Avila was wounded in just this way, as she describes:

"I see beside me, on my left, an angel in bodily form. He was not tall, but short, and very beautiful. It must be those who are called cherubim. In his hand I saw a long golden spear and at the end of the iron tip I seemed to see a point of fire. With this he seemed to pierce my heart several times so that it penetrated into my entrails. When he drew it out, I thought he was drawing them out with it and he left me completely afire with a great love for God…"(Life, chpt. 29.)

This same celestial visit was experienced by Padre Pio of Pietrelcina (1887 -1968), as he described in his letter to his spiritual director, Padre Agostino:

"I am led to manifest to you what happened to me on the evening of the 5th of this month and all day on the 6th."

"I am quite unable to convey to you what occurred during this period of utter torment. While I was hearing the boy's confessions on the evening of the 5th I was suddenly terrorized by the sight of a celestial person who presented himself to my mind's eye. He had in his hand a sort of weapon like a very long sharp-pointed steel blade which seemed to emit fire. At the very instant that I saw all this, I saw that person hurl the weapon into my soul with all his might. I cried out with difficulty and felt I was dying. I asked the boy to leave because I felt ill and no longer had the strength to continue."

"This agony lasted uninterruptedly until the morning of the 7th. I cannot tell you how much I suffered during this period of anguish. Even my entrails were torn and ruptured by the weapon, and nothing was spared. From that day on I have been mortally wounded. I feel in the depths of my soul a wound that is always open and which causes me continual agony…"(August 21, 1918.)

This wounding of the heart in Padre Pio is remarkably similar to that which was described by St. Teresa of Avila. As we have seen before, St. Francis of Assisi also received his wounds from the appearance of a majestic, celestial being.

In many cases, the transverberation of the heart directly precedes the impression of the Five Wounds. (Note: sometimes this transverberation is only felt internally and is not manifested on the outside of the body. In this case, the complete Five Wounds would app at at a later time. If the original transverberation did appear externally, then only the hand and foot wounds would manifest when the Sacred Stigmata appears, thus completing the major wounds of our Lord's Crucifixion). We must also realize that many stigmatized souls-such as St. Teresa of Avila-never receive all of the Five Wounds, but only receive a portion of them: the heart wound, the hand wounds, the crown of thorns, etc.

Although many a stigmatist receives the transverberation or the complete stigmata from the hands of a heavenly figure, nevertheless sometimes it is the Lord himself who visits the soul to wound the heart with His divine love. St. Gertrude the Great heard these words from our Lord before she was permanently inflicted: "I desire to pierce thy heart through and through so that the wound can never be healed."

Paradoxically, these wounds are pleasant and desirable to the victim, even though they are intensely painful:

"How sweet is that loving dart which, in wounding one with the incurable Wound of divine love, leaves him forever sick and with such a violent beating of the heart that it leads to death…"(Treatise on the Love of God, Book VIT, chpt. 10.)

Or again, the stigmatist St. Catherine of Siena (1347-80) had this to say:

"Oh, abyss of charity! Thou art a fire that ever burns but does not consume; a fire filled with joy, happiness and sweetness. To the heart which is wounded with this arrow all bitterness seems sweet and all heaviness is turned into lightness…"(Letter no. 123.)

The pain these mystics describe is not merely a pain of the body or senses; it is a pain that penetrates the interior of the soul, causing it to moan, but with heavenly splendor. According to St. Teresa, they are like intense longings for God, similar to the beloved spouse who awaits the bridegroom. In mystical language, this spouse is the chosen soul, and the Bridegroom is Jesus himself.

If these mystical wounds are intense enough, they will appear in the depths of the soul, or they could manifest themselves outside the body. Sometimes this transverberation or wound of the heart is called the "Seraph's assault," because, as St. John of the Cross reminds us, the soul is interiorly attacked by a Seraph who pierces the heart or soul with a fiery dart, wounding it permanently but with a sweet delight.

If this wound becomes even more intense and penetrates the body so roughly that external manifestations of the wounds become apparent, e victim is sealed with the visible stigmata. Padre Pio once experienced such a similar prelude to his visible marks, as we have seen:

"From Thursday evening until Saturday and also Tuesday, there is a painful tragedy for me. My heart, hands and feet seem to be pierced through by a sword. I feel great pain on this account…"(Letter to Padre Agostino, March 21, 1912.)

This description was certainly a prelude to the permanent visible stigmata that Padre was to receive on September 20, 1918, a mere six years later.

It must be repeated that these heavenly wounds usually occur because of intense impulses of love on the part of those who are wounded. Again, Padre Pio expresses this keen desire: "My heart wants more and more to experience any affliction whatever if this pleases Jesus" (Epistolario, August 19, 1910); "I am suffering and would like to suffer even more. I feel myself consumed and would like to be consumed even more" (May 6, 1913); "I want to suffer: This is what I long for" (July 27, 1918).

These desires are not aimed at suffering for its own sake-this would be pathetic and perhaps even pathological. No, they are impulses for a share in Christ's Passion: their redemptive and purifying values are what is at stake. Only then does suffering take on a truly meaningful experience that transcends all earthly values. It becomes a supernatural value that stores up treasure in heaven for those who seek God with all their hearts, souls and minds.

All of us can benefit from these merits that the suffering victim souls earn for our salvation on behalf of Jesus; thus, we must hold in awe their very mission of self-sacrifice through suffering out of love for God and His people. The stigmatist's love is a sacrificial love spilled out for every soul in need of God's mercy, for a brokenness that cries out for healing and reconciliation.

Sacred Stigmata

One of the most incredible mystical gifts ever given by God to some privileged souls is the **sacred stigmata**: the visible or invisible wounds of our Lord's Passion imprinted on the bodies of a few victim souls. These victims offer themselves up in union with Christ in order to make reparation for the sins of the world. According to Dr. A. Imbert-Gourbeyre, the noted Parisian scholar and expert on mystical theology, there have been three hundred twenty-one authentic stigmatics in Church history. (This study was done in 1894 and brought to light in a two-volume work called *La Stigmatization*; a number of authentic stigmatics have been identified since Dr. Imbert-Gourbeyre's study.) In his research, Dr. Imbert-Gourbeyre found sixty-two of the three hundred twenty-one stigmatics had either been beatified of canonized. Other interesting statistics about authentic stigmatics: One hundred stigmatics have had the side wound, twenty-two have had the wound on the left side of the body, and six have had the side wound on the right. A great number of victim souls bore the **invisible stigmata**: wounds of the Passion that are as real, painful, and permanent as those that are visible. (For a comprehensive study on this phenomenon, refer to the author's *They Bore Wounds of Christ: The Mystery of the Sacred Stigmata*.)

St. Francis of Assisi (1182-1226), founder of the Franciscans and one of the great saints of the Catholic Church, received the sacred stigmata on September 14, 1224, on Mount Alverna in northern Italy. These wounds remained with Francis until his death on

October 3, 1226. Many witnessed the reality of these wounds, including his close companions Brother Elias and St. Bonaventure. Francis is the first known authentic stigmatic in Church history, although there may have been others predating his time.

St. Clare of Montefalco (d. 1308) bore the painful stigmata of our Lord. After her death, it was revealed that the symbols of our Lord's Passion were found etched upon her heart: a crucifix the size of one's thumb, with the head of Christ leaning toward the right arm. Also found within her heart were images of the nails of the crucifixion, the crown of thorns, and a nerve that was in the shape of a lance.

St. Catherine of Siena (1347-1380), Dominican nun and Doctor of the Church, received the wounds of the stigmata during a visit to Pisa in 1375. The visible wounds became hidden after Catherine prayed to Jesus that He remove them so she would not be a subject of sensationalism for others. God granted her request; however, after she died the wounds reappeared. Many witnesses saw Catherine's stigmata when she was on her deathbed.

St. Lydwine of Schiedam (1380-1433) was one of the great victim souls in the history of the Church. She suffered innumerable afflictions, including the sacred stigmata, which she received sometime after 1407. These wounds were imparted upon Lydwine's body after she experienced a vision of heavenly angels, who came to pierce her soul with the Passion of our Lord. Lydwine carried the stigmata for the remainder of her life.

St. Rita of Cascia (1381-1457) received a thorn wound on her forehead after hearing a sermon in 1441 on the crown of thorns.

Many witnessed a mysterious light that came forth from this wound. Rita bore the stigma for the rest of her life.

Blessed Osanna of Mantua (1449-1505) was marked with the stigmata after she begged our Lord to let her share in His Passion. Her desire was to help atone for the sins of others (**co-redemptive** suffering). At first Osanna received the crown-of-thorn wounds; later on the five sacred wounds appeared upon her body. Although barely visible during her life, they appeared very distinct on her body after her death.

St. Teresa of Avila 1515-1582), Doctor of the Church and author of various mystical classics such as *Autobiography* (1565), *The Way of Perfection* (1573), and the *Interior Castle* (1577), received a stigma of the heart known. as **transverberation**. This wound, which was examined in 1872 by three physicians from the University of Salamanca, as verified as a puncture of the heart.

St. Catherine dei Ricci (1522-1590) began receiving visions of our Lord's Passion when she turned twenty. In 1542, Catherine began to receive the wounds of the stigmata . Her wounds were nearly complete: both feet, both hands, the side, and the crown-of thorn wounds. Every week from Thursday until 4:00 P.M. on Friday, Catherine relived the Passion of Christ. These sufferings continued for the next twelve years.

St. Mary Magdalen dei Pazzi (1566-1607) began receiving visions of Jesus and the Blessed Virgin Mary before her reception of the stigmata. It is claimed that her wounds emitted the sweet **odor of heaven**.

St. Rose of Lima (1586-1617) a Third Order Dominican, was given the five sacred wounds from our Lord during one of her many ecstatic states. In addition, it is believed that she received the crown-of-thorn wounds a short time later. Rose never did become a nun; rather, she chose to live at home and built a private haven for herself where she could pray, suffer, and do good works for others.

St. Margaret Mary Alacoque (1647-1690), mystic and author of *Jesus Reveals His Heart*, received the invisible stigmata from the Lord as well a the crown-of-thorn wounds. These facts were revealed in her *Autobiography*.

St. Veronica Giuliani (1660-1727), a Poor Clare nun, received the stigmata after her mother (Benedetta) had offered her up to the sufferings of Christ. According to one story, Benedetta as dying and entrusted each of her five daughters to one of the five sacred wounds. Veronica was entrusted to the wound below Christ's heart. On Good Friday in 1697, when she was thirty-seven years old, Veronica received the stigmata.

St. Mary Frances of the Five Wounds (1715-1791), member of the Order of Franciscans, received the stigmata in her hands, feet, and side. Her sufferings endured throughout the remainder of her life.

Venerable Anne Catherine Emmerich (1774-1824), controversial mystic and prophet from Germany, received the invisible stigmata after praying for hours before the cross in the Church of St. Lambert at Coesfeld. (At that time, Anne asked our Lord to share in His Passion as a sacrifice for the sake of her Augustinian convent.) On August 28, 1812-the Feast of St. Augustine-Anne was given a cross-shaped wound on her breast directly above her heart. Later that year, she received the complete stigmata, which became visible at this point. A medical examination in 1813 proved that her heart wound was three inches long. This wound was unusual in that it resembled the shape of a cross. The examinations went on for some five months. Doctors verified that real wounds did indeed appear on Anne's hands, feet, and side. The crusty blood was examined and proven to be from deep wounds whose cause was unexplainable by human standards.

Louise Lateau (1850-1883) was one of the most thoroughly examined stigmatics in Church history. She began to suffer the pains of the Passion for the first time on January 3, 1868, and continued until April 24, when blood issued forth from her side wound. On the following Friday, May 1, blood began to flow from the upper surface of her feet. On May 8, Louise received the wounds on her hands. Besides suffering the five sacred wounds, Louise also received the crown-of-thorn wounds. Examinations by medical authorities proved that there were twelve to fifteen circular marks around her head that looked like punctures and bled freely. According to a Dr. Lefebvre, one-time professor at the Catholic University in Louvain, Louise suffered at least eight hundred hemorrhages from her weekly Passion ecstasies.

St. Gemma Galgani (1878-1903) received the sacred stigmata on June 8, 1899. At this time, the Blessed Virgin Mary appeared to her along with her Son, Jesus. Gemma saw flames of fire issuing forth from our Lord's wounds, which suddenly appeared on her own body in the exact locations as the wounds of Christ. Not wanting to become a showpiece for others, Gemma asked our Lord to remove the visible wounds. Her request was granted. However, she did not really lose her wounds at all; rather, they became invisible and lasted for the next three years until her death.

Sister Josefa Menendez (1890-192 ,Coadjutrix Sister of the Society of the Sacred Heart of Jesus and author of *The Way of Divine Love*, received all the wounds of the stigmata over the last few years of her life. Jesus had chosen Josefa to be a **victim soul** for the sins of the world.

Marie-Rose Ferron (1902-1936), the first recognized (though controversial) stigmatic from the United States, was given the sacred wounds of Christ beginning in 1927. At that time, she first experienced the scourge marks. A few days later, the wounds on her hands appeared. By October of 1927, "Little Rose" received the foot wounds, and in November her heart became pierced. In January of 1928, Rose was given the crown-of-thorn wounds to complete her Passion. These wounds had been examined by many competent doctors throughout the course of her life. A number of photographs reveal Rose's wounds; especially vivid is a cordlike mark that wraps around Rose's forehead. Considered a controversial figure-partly because her bishop at the time was dubious of any extraordinary gifts or signs-her cause of canonization has never been officially introduced, although it has gathered great momentum in the past decades. Hundreds of testimonies have been written in support of Rose's authenticity, and current efforts to revive her cause are under way.

Sister Faustina Kowalska (1905-1938), a member of the Congregation of the Sisters of Our Lady of Mercy,was given the stigmata in April of 1936. Although invisible the wounds would remain with Faustina the rest of her relatively short life. This pious mystic is known for her brilliant spiritual work entitled *Divine Mercy in My Soul: The Diary*.

Berthe Petit (1870-1943) of Belgium was a Third Order Franciscan. This victim soul received the wounds of Christ beginning on December 29, 1930. Except for occasional moments, Berthe's wounds remained invisible.

Alexandrina da Costa (1904-1955) from Balasar in Portugal, became bedridden after she jumped from her bedroom window while trying to escape a rapist's attack. Thereafter, she offered her suffering to God as a victim of His divine love. Alexandrina received the visible stigmata and experienced the Passion ecstasies over one hundred eighty times in her life. These ecstasies were well-documented by various doctors and authorities of the Church. It is claimed that Alexandrina relived approximately forty different Passion scenes for every Passion experience.

Therese Neumann (1898-1962) of Konnersreuth, Bavaria, Germany, was one of the most gifted mystical souls in the history of the Church. During Lent in 1926, Therese received the sacred stigmata. These wounds would last until her death in 1962: a total of thirty-six years, which is one of the longest time periods that anyone has ever borne the stigmata (Padre Pio holds the record: fifty years!). Therese's stigmata was one of the most complete among stigmatics as well. Besides the five sacred wounds, she bore eight to nine crown-of-thorn wounds (beginning on November 5,1926), the shoulder wound (March,1929), the flagellation marks (Good Friday,1929), and even shed tears of blood frequently. Examinations proved that there were 45 distinguishable marks of the Passion on Therese's body: 2 foot wounds, 2 hand wounds, 1 wound near the heart, 30 scourge marks, 1 shoulder wound, and 9 circular head wounds. Bedridden for a good portion of her life, Therese relived her Passion ecstasies on a weekly basis from Thursdays to Fridays. This occurred on an average of half the weeks throughout each year. It has been estimated that she suffered the entire Passion mystery some seven hundred fifty times!

Adrienne von Speyr (1902-1967), a Swiss layperson and Protestant convert, became a doctor and prolific writer. She bore the invisible stigmata, which was imprinted on her body in the spring of 1941. By July of 1942, Adrienne's wounds became visible, although they were small compared to those of other stigmatics and only appeared on the days of her Passion ecstasies. Adrienne was an enormously gifted writer and theologian. Her close friend and mentor, Father Hans Urs von Balthasar, kept track of her works and published several of them before his death in 1988. The number of written works that Adrienne produced is staggering: 10 complete books in manuscript form; close to 30 commentaries on Sacred Scripture; 9 published articles; 12 volumes of "posthumous" works; and 24 other theological writings, making a grand total of some 85 separate works!

Padre Pio of Pietrelcina (1887-1968), who lived at Our Lady of Grace Friary in San Giovanni Rotondo, near Foggia, Italy, for over fifty years, is known for a remarkable distinction unique in the history of the Church: This Franciscan friar bore the five sacred wounds of Christ for over half a century-from September 20, 1918, until his death on September 23, 1968! Nobody in Church history even comes close to this record. (The lay Franciscan stigmatic Therese Neumann probably holds that distinction for women: thirty-six years.) Miraculously, Padre Pio's , wounds completely disappeared the last few days of his life. It was as if God had taken away his wounds because his mission had finally ended. Perhaps the disappearance of the wounds was also another extraordinary sign from God that they were genuine.

Marthe Robin (1902-1981), a Third Order Franciscan from France, received the sacred stigmata on October 4, 1930, after years of suffering for others. Marthe also received the crown-of thorn wounds. Her Passion ecstasies-like those of most of the authentic stigmatics-occurred every week from Thursday through Friday.

Incorruptibility

Now we turn to another amazing gift that God bestows upon certain privileged souls: the gift of **incorruptibility**. The supernatural wonder of incorruptibility involves the total or partial preservation of the body or parts thereof, long after one has died-in some cases, even hundreds of years later. There are over a hundred cases of authentic incorruptibility since the Middle Ages, and evidence for such authenticity is overwhelming: Most of these one hundred cases involve preserved bodily parts or entire bodies that are still kept in various churches throughout Europe. Most of these incorruptible remains have been viewed by hundreds of thousands throughout Europe. Furthermore, the bodies have been thoroughly examined by medical doctors, anatomists, and scientists, thus making their authenticity beyond dispute.

The incorrupt skull of St. Agatha (d. 251) is kept in a reliquary at Catania, Sicily, Italy, where it is exposed on occasion for the veneration of the faithful. Agatha was martyred for not giving up her virginity to Quintianus, a Roman magistrate under, the Emperor Diocletian. Her punishment was very severe: scourging, burning, and the cutting off of her breasts.

The body of St. Clare of Montefalco (d. 1308), a victim soul who bore the stigmata, was found to be incorrupt years after her death. To this day, one can visit the saint and view her remains at the Church of the Holy Cross in Montefalco, Italy.

St. Francis of Paola (1416-1507), the "Wonder Worker," was attributed with so many miracles that the faithful recognized his sanctity early in life. For fifty-five years after his death, Francis' body remained perfectly preserved. In 1562, the Huguenots burned the remains in a defiant act against the Catholic faith. Nevertheless, some of his bones were discovered, and they are currently preserved in the Sanctuary of Paola.

It is believed that the body of St. Charles Borromeo (1538- 1684) was found in a perfect state of preservation and continues to remain incorrupt to this day. However, his remains were embalmed shortly after his death. The relics of St. Charles Borromeo can be found in the Cathedral of Milan, Italy.

The incorrupt heart of St. Vincent de Paul (1580-1660), founder of the Sisters of Charity, can be found at the Convent of the Sisters of Charity, also at the Rue du Bac.

A gifted servant of God, Blessed Anna Maria Taigi (1769-1837) was blessed with many mystical gifts, including supernatural visions and prophecies. In 1855-eighteen years after her death-Anna's body was removed to another resting place in Rome. During this time, it was noticed that her body was incorrupt. Since then, her remains have decomposed.

The body of St. Catherine Laboure of the Miraculous Medal (1806-1876) was found to be incorrupt fifty-six years after her burial. Later on, her remains had to be preserved by artificial means. Her body can still be seen in a glass reliquary beneath the side altar in the Chapel of the Apparitions at the Rue du Bac in Paris, France.

Another bodily phenomenon is that of **restoration to a youthful beauty** after one has died. This occurred to St. Germaine Cousin (1579-1601), who was an abused and sickly child. Germaine was born with physical deformities, and she had several repulsive body sores that made even her father and stepmother ashamed of her. Decades after her death-in 1644-the local townspeople of Pibrac, France, decided to bury a distant relative of Germaine's (Edualde) near the saint's body. After accidentally digging up Germaine's grave, they discovered a beautiful young girl under the ground, whose body lay in a perfect state of preservation. In addition to this miraculous wonder, it is said that the flowers placed upon Germain's head over thirty years earlier still retained a fresh, fragrant smell.

Additional Information

How was this extraordinary miracle of incorruptibility first discovered? In one sense, it was really accidental. For hundreds of years, it has been the practice of the Church to exhume the body of a potential candidate for sainthood, thus enabling him to be examined years after his death and original burial. (Many holy souls have been known to emit a heavenly perfume from their bodies long after they've gone; and many before have been found to be incorruptible. So, the practice continues.)

One practical reason for exhuming the body is that it had long been a practice to divide and distribute parts of the saint's body to many different churches throughout Christian world; in this way, the faithful would be allowed to venerate them by paying visits and praying before their remains in the altars or in the crypts. An example of this is with Therese Neumann. Plans are currently underway to remove her remains from the cemetery in Konnersreuth in order to have her placed under the side altar of St. Therese of Lisieux inside the St. Lawrence Church. This is being done in order to accommodate the large groups of pilgrims who visit the town annually. It had also been Therese's wish long before she died, since she so loved the Little Flower.

Another reason for the examination of saint's bodies is that, unfortunately, relics were frequently stolen by grave-robbers and over-zealous souls who sometimes sold the precious remains for huge profits. In order to be certain that the remains were intact (or that they were even at a particular site at all), the Church found it necessary to verify if the saint was indeed still where he or she was originally buried.

So many factors had contributed to the exposure and/or removal of the bodies of the saints who had died long ago. Today, the Process for Beatification and Canonization can take decades to finish before a candidate is declared a saint. Therefore, plenty of time will have elapsed for evidence of incorruptibility to be affirmed.

Let us now examine more than 100 authenticated cases that claim incorruptibility in the bodies of God's holy souls.

The body of the Dominican stigmatist, St. Catherine of Siena (1347-80) was found to be incorruptible, and her head can still be seen today in the Basilica of Sts. Catherine and Dominic in Siena, Italy. While in Siena, this author has also seen Catherine's finger preserved behind a glass encasing (although the skin is wrinkled and discolored, nevertheless this relic is fully formed; even her nail is still present!). The rest of her body is in safe keeping in Rome, where she had died.

St. Clare of Montefalco (1268-1308), Augustinian nun of heroic virtue, continues to mystify the faithful. Besides her body being incorrupt, this stigmatized saint has an image of the Crucifix imprinted in her heart. This relic has been examined and verified by authorities in the Church. She can be seen in the Church of the Holy Cross on Montefalco.

A thorn wound has been observed in the preserved body of St. Rita of Cascia (1381-1457). The Lord granted her a share in His Passion after she offered herself up to share in His sufferings. Her intact body-only slightly discolored after more than five centuries-can be seen in a glass case at the Basilica of St. Rita in Cascia, Italy. There are reports that her eyes have opened and closed several times over the years, and her body (according to eyewitnesses) has moved more than once.

The heart of the great St. Teresa of Avila (1515-82) was found to be preserved upon examination in 1872. This relic appears to be pierced with the wound of divine love, described once by Teresa herself in her autobiography (Life). Part of her remain were found to be still incorrupt after the last exhumation in 1914.

The Basilica of Prato, Italy, holds the incorruptible body of St. Catherine dei Ricci (1522-90), stigmatist who was inflicted with the Five Wounds of Christ, as well as the crown of thorn wounds.

Though darkened with time, her body is available for the veneration of the faithful below the main altar of the basilica.

The partially preserved remains of stigmatist St. Rose of Lima (1586-1617), Patroness of the Americas, are occasionally exposed to the faithful in the Church of Santo Domingo in Lima, Peru. Part of her body rests here, while the remainder of her relics is located in a small church close to where Rose had once lived.

St. Veronica Giuliani (1660-1727), stigmatist who carried the Five Wounds of Christ as well as the crown of thorn wounds, was incorrupt for many years. Later, when the Tiber River overflowed and atur ted her body, it was destroyed. Yet her heart was preserved, and mains intact to this day in the Capuchin Monastery at Citta di Castello, here her skull is also preserved.

Blessed Osanna of Mantua (1449-1505), like St. Catherine of Siena, received the Sacred Stigmata but requested that the Lord make them invisible, a request that was later granted. Osanna' body, displayed three time a year in the Cathedral of Mantua, is still well-preserved. Like St. Catherine, Osanna's stigmata later reappeared her body, visible for all to see.

The question must be asked: why does incorruptibility occur? How can it possibly benefit those who have died, let alone those who are still living? One explanation is that God has left a sign for the faithful, indicating how He is Master of both body and soul, before and after death. Another reason is to reaffirm the teachings of St. Paul on the reallty of the bodily resurrection the faithful will one day encounter:

"There are celestial bodies and there are terrestrial bodies; but the glory of the celestial is one thing, and the glory of the terrestrial is another. There is one glory of the sun, and another glory of the moon, and another glory of the stars; for star differs from star in glory. So it is with the resurrection of the dead. What is sown is perishable, what is raised is imperishable ... (1 Cor 15:40-42).

Our bodies will be changed into spiritual bodies not subject to corruption: "this perishable nature must put on the imperishable" (1 Cor 15:53). But these risen bodies will nevertheless remain true bodies: "It is sown a physical body, it is raised a spiritual body" (1 Cor 15:44). One is reminded of this fact through the incident of our Lord's risen appearance to St. Thomas: "See my hands and my feet, that it is I myself; handle me, and see; for a spirit has not flesh and bones" (Lk 24:39); or the Transfiguration narrative: "And he was transfigured before them and his face shone like the sun, and his garments became white as light. And behold, there appeared to them Moses and Elijah talking with him" (Mt 17:2-3).

As incredible as incorruptibility may appear, it really ought not to cause us to doubt, for with God all things are possible. In fact, this phenomenon is nothing compared to the hope for what is yet to come:

"What no eye has seen, nor ear heard, nor the heart of man conceived, what God has prepared for those who love him" (1 Cor 2:9).

Luminous Effluvia

An extraordinary physical phenomenon called **luminosity**, or **luminous effluvia**, has been observed in many of the saints. This phenomenon includes a bright light that seems to surround the bodies of the privileged souls. Sometimes, this light appears as a type of halo around the head; with some stigmatists, a bright light is emitted from the wounds of the victim soul.

One of the best-known examples of luminosity occurred In the New Testament during the Transfiguration: "And after six days Jesus took with him Peter and James and John his brother, and led them up a high mountain apart. And he was transfigured before them, and his face shone like the sun, and his garments became white as light" (Mt 17:1-2).

A Father Nicholas Lannoy once saw a brilliant flame of fire hovering over the head of St. Ignatius of Loyola (1491-1556). This occurred during a Mas that Ignatius had celebrated in the presence of Father Lannoy.

St. Alphonsus Liguori (1696-1787) was once reading and meditating before the Blessed Sacrament when members of his Order entered the dark church. They described a glowing light that came from Alphonsus' eyebrow, illuminating the book he was reading.

St. Julie Billiart (1751-1816) was seen with a halo of light around her head whenever she went into an ecstatic state. Some even stated that Julie's face would frequently take on a Christ-like appearance.

It is said that St. Peter Julian Eymard (1811-1868) was seen by a Mother Superior to give off a supernatural glow: "I turned around and was astonished to see the priest's face all alight with beauty. In the visitor's parlor he had seemed sad but here in the chapel he was transfigured with the smile of an angel…" Others claimed that when Peter said Mass, his body would often take on a luminous glow.

St. John Bosco (1815-1888) was known for his many supernatural gifts. One witness named Philip Rinaldi (1856-1931) told of a time when he went to John Bosco for confession. In a small dark sacristy behind the altar, he noticed a halo glowing around the saint's head. This same witness also saw Don Bosco, as he is popularly called, illuminate during times of deep prayer.

It is believed that the famed holy man from Montreal, Blessed Andre Bessette (1845-1937), was seen by many with a luminous glow about his body. The descriptions of this phenomenon are many: **supernatural radiance** , **illumination**, an **aureole**, **transfiguration**, etc.

Don Luigi Orione (1872-1940), beatified by Pope John Paul II in October, 1980, claimed he saw on more than one occasion Pope Pius X "illumined with a supernatural light."

St. Maximilian Kolbe (1894-1941), the priest who died in place of a family man who was imprisoned in Auschwitz during Hitler's persecutions, was seen by Brother Luke Kuszba in an illuminated state, glowing with an "unearthly radiance." This luminosity occurred during Maximilian's visits before the chapel tabernacle several times each day.

Father Aloysius Ellacuria (1905-1981) was known for his extraordinary gifts: ecstasies, bilocation, levitation, and the gift of perfume. A Brother Salvatore Azzarello once claimed to have seen a luminous glow surrounding Aloysius at a sister's home. Salvatore's own sister, Antonia More, reported that she saw a light around Aloysius when he was deeply immersed in prayer. Another witness, a priest who had not seen Aloysius for thirty years-as told by Charles Carpenter, who was Father Aloysius' former secretary-declared that he saw him at a meeting radiating with a supernatural glow on his face.

Heavenly Aromas

It is said that Blessed Claritus (d. 1348), an Augustinian from Florence, Italy, was a great servant to the nuns at the convent there known as Chiarito. After his death, many experienced a sweet, heavenly perfume coming from Claritus' grave anytime a nun was close to death.

The body of St. Rita of Cascia (1381-1457), stigmatized in 1441, gave off a sweet aroma that invaded her small convent cell. Many witnesses experienced the heavenly perfume that remained in her quarters even when she was not physically present.

St. Teresa of Avila (1515-1582), mystic and Doctor of the Church, was known to emit a sweet perfume from her body throughout her life and well after her death. The heavenly aroma was still evident during the examination of Teresa's remains on July 4, 1583, and again in 1914.

The body of St. Catherine dei Ricci (1522-1590), the Dominican stigmatic, allegedly had a flowery scent at the time of her death.

It is claimed that the body of St. Mary Magdalen dei Pazzi (1566-1607) gave off a sweet scent from her grave. She was a victim soul and stigmatic, having entered the Carmelite Order in 1582.

St. Veronica Giuliani (1660-1727), stigmatized in 1697, was known to have emitted a sweet fragrance from her wounds that penetrated the entire confines of her convent.

It is said that Marie-Rose Ferron (1902-1936), the American stigmatic known as "Little Rose," gave off a sweet aroma from her wounds. This scent was noticed by hundreds of her admirers.

Alexandrina da Costa (1904-1955), victim soul and stigmatic from Portugal, suffered more than one hundred eighty Passio ecstasies throughout her life. After she died, it is said that her ashes continued to emit a heavenly perfume to those who visited her grave.

Padre Pio of Pietrelcina (1887-1968), stigmatic from 1918 until his death, emitted a sweet heavenly perfume from the wounds of his stigmata. Many have claimed that the rose petals on his tomb remained with a sweet smell for many months after they were removed.

Mysterious Oils

St. Nicholas of Myra (d. c. 350), the legendary figure who is celebrated today as Santa Claus, was laid to rest in the Basilica of St. Nicholas in Bari, Italy. It is said that his preserved bones have continued to emit a liquid secretion on various occasions for over sixteen hundred years.

'It is reported that the bones of the Apostle St. Andrew, believed to be preserved in Amalfi, Italy, emits a mysterious oil known in mystical circles as "manna." Although the anniversary of St. Andrew is officially celebrated on November 30, this miraculous oil has appeared each year on January 28 since 1846, the year when Andrew's bones were discovered in a crypt beneath the floor of the basilica in which the crypt is now kept.

Resurrections

It is claimed that St. Helena (250-330), mother of Emperor Constantine and finder of the true cross in Jerusalem, had performed a test to determine the authenticity of the cross of the crucifixion. When she discovered the holy cross, two other crosses were found together as well. Unable to determine which one held the body of our Lord, she touched each cross to a corpse. Only one of the crosses revived the dead man, thereby indicating its authenticity.

St. Ambrose (340-397), Bishop of Milan and Doctor of the Church, raised from the dead a boy named Pansopius. In Florence, Ambrose had once freed the young man from an unclean spirit.

St. Patrick of Ireland (389-461) is reported to have raised at least thirty-nine people from the dead.

Tradition tell us that St. Benedict of Nursia (480-547), the Father of Western Monasticism, had raised two people from the dead: One was a monk who had been crushed during construction work on the Monastery of Monte Cassino; the other was a dead child.

A legend claims that St. Winifred (d. c. 650) was beheaded for refusing the sexual advances of a prince named Caradoc. It is said that her head was miraculously restored as she came back to life. Winifred later became a nun and lived a number of years after her resurrection. A fountain at Holywell-which reportedly started flowing at the moment of Winifred's beheading-is still visited by many pilgrims.

St. Stanislaus of Cracow (1030-1079), bishop and martyr, reportedly raised Peter Miles back to life. One story claims that Peter had been falsely accused of a crime, which went with him to the grave. After his life wa restored, Peter claimed to have been in purgatory. Stanislaus gave Peter a choice of two conditions after his return to this earthly life: to live on where he was or to return to purgatory finish his purification there, and be guaranteed eternal life. Peter chose the latter. He lay down in his grave, and quickly his body decomposed to the condition it had been when his grave had been opened!

St. Malachy of Ireland (1095-1148) Archbishop of Armagh and famous prophet of the Catholic Church, raised to life a woman who had died before he was able to give her the Sacrament of Anointing. After praying all night for the woman, she miraculously came back to life.

St. Dominic (1170-1221), founder of the Dominicans and one of the great preachers of the Catholic Church, allegedly brought back to life a young man named Neapolion, who died by falling from a horse.

St. Anthony of Padua (1195-1231), miracle worker and Doctor of the Church, was known to have raised dozens of people from the dead. One of them was a small infant, who rose after Anthony made the Sign of the Cross. This occurred when the mother of the baby promised Anthony that she would give the child's weight in grain if he were only restored. (This story accounts for the tradition known as "St. Anthony's Bread": giving alms to the poor in petition or thanksgiving to St. Anthony.) In another case, it is said that Anthony raised to life a man who needed to testify to Anthony's father's innocence in a murder trial.

St. Elizabeth of Hungary (1207-1231) raised a number of people from the dead: three children, an adolescent, and a stillborn infant.

Legends surrounding the life of St. Hyacinth (1185-1257) claim that he raised fifty people from the dead at Cracow and restored another seventy-two who were close to death.

Many people had brought the dead to the body of St. Philip Benizi (1233-1285), General of the Servite Order, believing that his intercession would restore lost life. It is claimed that Philip once brought back to life a mutilated girl who had been attacked by a wolf. As soon as the girl's body was placed near St. Philip's, her life was restored with all her bodily parts intact!

St. Agnes of Montepulciano (1268-1317) raised to life a child who had drowned and whose body was found floating in the water.

Blessed Margaret of Castello (1287-1320), the blind hunchback known for her deep faith in God and charity toward others, raised a dead man and two children back to life.

St. Peregrine Laziozi (1260-1345) is said to have raised many people back to life. An Italian Servite, Peregrine was known for his preaching and miracles.

St. Catherine of Siena (1347-13 0), famed stigmatist and Doc tor of the Church, raised her mother, Mona Lapa, back to life. Catherine pleaded for this favor from God, as Mona had died without receiving the Last Sacraments.

St. Catherine of Sweden (1331-1381), daughter of St. Bridget of Sweden (1303-1373), reportedly rai d two men from the dead. It is also claimed that St. Bridget herself had brought several people back from the dead.

One of the great miracle workers is St. Vincent Ferrer (1350-1419), famed p r f the Dominican Order. It is believed that WI cent rai ed at least twenty-eight persons from the dead. One of these was a child who had been chopped up and roasted by his mother in a rage of madness.

In Lagny-sur-Marn, near Paris, France, it is believed that St. Joan of Arc 412-1431), the Maid of Orleans, once raised a stillborn infant back to life in order that he may be baptized.

It is believed that St. Bernardine of Siena (1380-1444), famed Franciscan preacher, restored to life four different people. One of them-a man named Blasio Massei- returned to tell about his visits to heaven, hell, and purgatory.

Tradition holds that St. Colette (1381-1447) had raised a nun back to life who had passed away without being absolved of her sins. Another legend claims that Colette raised a child from the dead who was already buried; she has also been credited with giving back life to many stillborn infants.

Blessed Colomba of Rieti (1468-1501), a Third Order Dominican, raised several people back to life.

St. Francis of Paola (1416-1507), miracle worker and mystical wonder, allegedly raised his dead nephew back to life so that he could become a monk. Earlier, this nephew's mother had refused to grant him this permission.

The Jesuit St. Francis Xavier (1506-1552), one of the greatest missionaries in Church history, reportedly raised a boy back to life who had been wrapped in a shroud. (It was estimated that he had lain in in this condition for over twenty-four hours.)

The founder of the Society of Jesus (Jesuits), St. Ignatius of Loyola (1491-1556), raised from the dead a man named Lessani. It was claimed that Lessani had hanged himself after losing a lawsuit.

St. Louis Bertrand (1526-1581), Dominican missionary to South America, is said to have raised two people back to life, and another thirteen persons were raised through his intercession after his own death.

St. Teresa of Avila (1515-1582), reformer of the Carmelite Order and first woman Doctor of the Church, was said to have raised her six-year-old nephew Gonzalo from the dead.

The Franciscan St. Felix of Cantalice (515-1587) raised from death a child and gave him back to his mother.

St. Philip Neri (1515-1595), founder of the Confraternity of the Most Holy Trinity, raised fourteen-year-old Paolo Massimi back to life. The young boy had revealed to Philip that he neglected to confess a serious sin before his death. After his confession before the saint, Paolo died again in his arms.

After his death, it is claimed that through the intercession of Blessed Sebastian of Apparizio (1502-1600), Franciscan lay brother and missionary to Mexico, eight children were brought back to life.

St. Francis Solanus (1549-1610), Franciscan missionary to South America, allegedly restored the life of five-year-old Maria Monroy, who had died from a fall that fractured her skull.

Through the intercession of St. Rose of Lima (1586-1617) after her death, it is claimed that two people were raised from the dead. Rose was a stigmatic and is patroness of South America.

Father Vincent Bernedo (562-f619), Spanish missionary of the Dominican Order, gave new life to a widow who was about to be buried. Also, during one of his missionary journeys to South America, Father Bernedo raised to life an Indian boy who had drowned.

St. Martin de Porres (1579-1639) of Lima, Peru, friend of St. Rose of Lima and founder of hospitals and orphanages, reportedly raised from death a fellow monk and a dog.

It is said that St. Marianne de Jesus of Quito (1618-1645), vic tim soul from Ecuador, brought back to life her own niece, who died from a head injury after being kicked by a mule. Marianne also raised a woman back to life who had been thrown over a cliff by an abusive husband.

St. Francis Jerome (1642-1716), famed Jesuit preacher, allegedly raised to life a man and a baby.

It is said that St. Paul of the Cross (1694-1775), founder of the Passionist Order, brought back to life a child who had fallen out of a church window and met his death on the ground below.

St. John Bosco (1815-1888), founder of the Society of St. Francis de Sales (the Salesians), was known to have raised two boys from death. One was a fifteen-year-old named Charles, in 1849. After Charles made a final confession before St. John, the boy died in peace. Tradition also claims that Don Bosco (as he is also known) raised a dead ox and a hen back to life.

After his own death, St. Charbel Makhlouf (1828-1898), a Lebanese hermit, interceded to restore to life a two-year-old child.

Many medical authorities have testified that the German victim soul and stigmatic Therese Neumann (1898-1962) clinically "died" each time she experienced her weekly Passion ecstasy. Yet soon after her heart had topped beating and all vital signs of life had disappeared, she miraculously came to, and all her vital signs were restored to normal! This life-and-death cycle was witnessed by thousands during more than seven hundred ecstasies during the years 1926 to 1962.

It is claimed by some that after his own death, Padre Pio of Pietrelcina (1887-1968), stigmatic and one of the most gifted souls in the history of the Church, reportedly interceded for a dead man, whose life was later restored.

About the Author

My background as a publisher author is wide and diverse. Here is a general bibliography of my works and the television shows I have appeared on concerning some of those works:

The nationally-published books to my credit:

"Questions And Answers: The Gospel of Matthew"

"Questions And Answers: The Gospel of Mark"

"Questions And Answers: The Gospel of Luke"

"Questions And Answers: The Gospel of John"

(All published with Baker Book House of Grand Rapids, MI).

On the more scholarly side, I have written the following works:

"They Bore The Wounds Of Christ: The Mystery Of The Sacred Stigmata"

"The Making Of Saints"

"Voices, Visions, & Apparitions"

"Patron Saints"

(All published with Our Sunday Visitor of Huntington, IN).

One of my recent eBooks now in print with Amazon Kindle ("The Complete Guide To Demonology & The Spirits of Darkness") received the Imprimatur after a prior review by the former Bishop Elden Curtiss of the Diocese of Helena, Montana. Released in December 2015, it is 450 pages long.

My Religious eBooks In Print

My eBooks with Amazon Kindle:

"Demonology & The Spirits of Darkness: History Of Demons" (Volume 1: 184 pages)

"Demonology & The Spirits of Darkness: The Spiritual Warfare" (Volume 2: 135 pages)

"Demonology & The Spirits of Darkness: Possession & Exorcism" (Volume 3: 127 pages)

"Demonology & The Spirits of Darkness: Dictionary of Demonology" (Volume 4: 252 pages)

"Demonology & The Spirits of Darkness: A Catholic Perspective" (Volume 5: 450 pages)

"Demonology & The Spirits of Darkness: Infestation, Oppression, & Demonic Activity" (Volume 6: 130 pages)

"Demonology & The Spirits of Darkness: History Of The Occult" (Volume 7: 70 pages)

"Demonology & The Spirits of Darkness: Witchcraft & Sorcery" (Volume 8: 93 pages)

"Demonology & The Spirits of Darkness: Evil Spirits In The Bible" (Volume 9: 43 pages)

"Demonology & The Spirits of Darkness: The Exorcist" (Volume 10: 95 pages)

"Demonology & The Spirits of Darkness: Types Of Demons & Evil Spirits" (Volume 11: 89 pages)

"Demonology & The Spirits of Darkness: Temptations Of The Devil" (Volume 12: 48 pages)

"Voices, Visions, & Apparitions: Voices From Heaven" (Volume 1, 25 pages)

"Voices, Visions, & Apparitions: Heaven, Hell, & Purgatory" (Volume 2, 25 pages)

"Ghosts Poltergeists and Haunting Spirits: A Religious Perspective" (141 pages)

"The Mystery of the Sacred Stigmata: My Interviews With Padre Pio's Spiritual Advisors" (Volume 1, 25 pages)

"The Mystery of the Sacred Stigmata: My Personal Interview With The Vice Postulator For The Cause Of Beatification Of Therese Neumann" (Volume 2, 29 pages)

"Voices, Visions, & Apparitions: Heaven, Hell, & Purgatory" (25 pages)

"Voices, Visions, & Apparitions: Voices From Heaven" (33 pages)

"Voices, Visions, & Apparitions: Angels & Saints" (46 pages)

"Angels In The Bible: The Bible Trivia Series" (Volume 1) (52 pages)

"The Gospel of Matthew: The Bible Trivia Series (Volume 2)" (127 pages)

"The Gospel of Matthew: The Bible Trivia Series (Volume 3)" (147 pages)

"1,130 Bible Trivia Questions! The Bible Trivia Series (Volume

4)" (242 pages)

"30 Christmas Poems To Make Your Holidays Bright!: Special Poems For The Holiday Season" (32 pages)

"300 Christmas Trivia Facts You Might Not Know!: Customs, Traditions, Celebrations" (18 pages)

"Do You Really Know Jesus Christ? Questions About The Biblical Jesus" (104 pages)

Educational Background

A Bachelor of Arts degree in Secondary Education from the University of Montana, Missoula, Montana (1984). My major is English with minors in Religious Studies & History.

Television Appearances

Television Appearances as a guest interviewee for my works: "The History Channel," "The Phil Donahue Show," "The Leeza Show," and "EWTN: Mother Angelica Live!" (3 times as a guest).

Links To My YouTube Videos For My National Television Appearances

https://www.youtube.com/channel/UCmrULjCTF4IjSLwynLYO3fQ

Links To My Writing Sites

http://www.amazon.com/-/e/B001KIZJS4

https://www.facebook.com/mike.freze1

Made in the USA
Monee, IL
29 August 2020